Niccolò Paganini
1782-1840

Marina Piccinini

24 Caprices

Arranged for Flute by
Marina Piccinini

Edited by
Scott Wollschleger
Jordan Rae Borg

ED 30116

www.schott-music.com

Mainz · London · Madrid · New York · Paris · Prague · Tokyo · Toronto
© 2014 SCHOTT MUSIC CORPORATION, New York · Printed in USA

Contents

Preface

Paganini's unusual dedication of the *24 Caprices "Alli Artisti,"* "To the Artists," marks the emergence of the artist as an independent, significant member of society. Paganini's perception of the musician's role was both idealistic and pragmatic; his vision coupled a commitment to his craft with a fine psychological understanding of the listener's needs. The *Caprices* are Paganini's exploration of the possibilities of high instrumental virtuosity – not only as a tool for great artistic achievement, but also as a medium for musicians willing to delve further into the mysteries of art. Along with Liszt's *Études d'exécution transcendante* and the Chopin *Études*, the great pianist Alfred Cortot (1877-1962) would later proclaim Paganini's *Caprices* "as inaccessible to the musician without virtuosity as they are to the virtuoso without musicianship."

Since their first publication in 1820, the *Caprices* have – for violinists – spurred creative exploration, pushed the limits of the instrument, opened up a new dimension in musical language, and encouraged the development of new pedagogical approaches, each caprice establishing a particular technical discipline – a masterly practical lesson of instrumental playing. But the *Caprices'* uncommon inspirational potential has also catapulted beyond the violin to other composers and instrumental virtuosos. For the flutist*, they present a stimulating challenge for development owing to musical language that demands emotional expression through technical perfection of phrasing, flexibility of embouchure, breath control, digital dexterity, and precise articulation.

A facsimile edition of the autograph – housed in the Archivio Storico di Casa Ricordi and issued by Ricordi in 1974 – served as my primary source in identifying correct accidentals and authentic articulations and tempi, details which have frequently been overlooked in subsequent editions. However, in embracing the idiomatic nature of transcribing, I allowed myself to modify several passages and techniques enabling the flute to capture the original feeling, expression, and phrasing in its own natural manner.

Thank you to Dr. JeeYoung Rachel Choe for her patience and painstaking support in transcribing my original manuscript into a legible version, and to Norman Ryan and Scott Wollschleger at Schott New York for their willingness to accommodate my many wishes and their steadfast commitment to producing such a beautiful and tasteful new publication.

Marina Piccinini
Vienna, 2014

*A recording of these flute transcriptions is available on AVIE Records: *Paganini 24 Capricci*, arranged for flute and played by Marina Piccinini AV2284. More information can be found at www.avie-records.com.

About the Caprices

Caprice No. 1: Andante

Despite the intimidating fast notes, the first caprice should be approached in a graceful, lyrical, and buoyant manner, accentuating the harmonic progression in an elegant, flowing line. To this end, I have chosen to slur the first group of notes to provide an impetus for light, upward motion. I then use a light, soft articulation for the second set of four notes, following the natural flow and shape of the beats.

Departing from the original ending's dynamics (the last two measures are marked *forte*), I have chosen to fade away at the conclusion while additionally challenging the flutist with the incorporation of harmonics on the high E's, extending the gentle nature of this caprice.

Caprice No. 2: Moderato

The original violin part calls for a *spiccato* articulation, a string technique which elicits a soft but consistent tone. Therefore I have added tenuto marks over the *detaché* notes, allowing the flutist to follow the melodic line with a slightly longer articulation. This will result in a gentle, nostalgic feeling which mirrors Paganini's *dolce* marking. Using support, focus on the lower notes and – by allowing the lips greater flexibility – the high and low notes and intervallic jumps will complement each other, following the natural contours of the melodic line.

Caprice No. 3: Sostenuto-Presto-Sostenuto

Play through the octave jumps using a dark, strong tone to imitate the dense sound of violin octaves. The grace notes should be quick and deliberate, the line *ben legato e posato*, and the trills held for the full value without a *nachschlag*. In the Presto section, finger dexterity and smoothness are further challenged by the extreme *legato* phrases. Pay attention to the phrase markings, as these will facilitate insightful breathing decisions and help to ground the fingers.

Caprice No. 4: Maestoso

The spirit of this caprice is romantic, grandiose, majestic, and *triste*. However, it should be played with a powerful and deep sonority throughout, even in the *piano* passages. The grace notes in the melodic line hint at the original chordal sound achieved by the double stops of the violin. Therefore, play them as rhythmically close as possible to the melodic note using extreme *legato*.

Caprice No. 5: Agitato

The fifth caprice offers ample opportunity for the flutist to perfect double-tonguing. Articulation should be light and soft throughout, as in the bouncy violin technique *saltato*. Use the airstream to propel the speed, being conscious of finger-tongue coordination. To achieve clarity and speed, practice each 16th note with two articulations ("TK" per note) so that the tongue stays fast and the fingers have more time to secure the tactile element.

Caprice No. 6: Lento

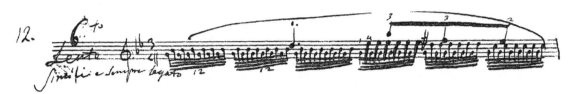

On the violin, Paganini evokes a mysterious and spectral atmosphere, combining a sustained melodic line with a hushed tremolo accompaniment. As this is an impossible feat on the traditional flute, it is left up to us to create the illusion of a two-part texture. To achieve this, always play the main melodic note with a light but clear articulation and hold on slightly to the principal note before slurring into the tremolo (without a new articulation). The tremolo should also be played slightly softer than the melodic note. Although Paganini indicates a rhythmic subdivision of the tremolo (see the example), I have chosen to leave it open. This allows the flutist to change the speed of the tremolo depending on the direction of the melody, emphasizing the flow of the harmonic accompaniment.

Caprice No. 7: Posato
As indicated by the title, this caprice should begin with a steady and vibrant rhythmic feeling, exuding vigor and energy in the phrasing and articulation. To achieve the brilliance and speed of the violin, it is important that the 32nd note passages (beginning at m.16) have a light yet clear articulation that contrasts with the longer, more *legato* phrasing found elsewhere in this caprice.

Caprice No. 8: Maestoso
The majestic quality of this caprice is achieved from the very first grace notes by using strong breath support, breaking the octave jumps while controlling and modulating the pitch and quality of the sound. Beginning at m.8 and continuing in the later corresponding passages, accentuate the melodic line by sustaining the principal note slightly longer, then by playing the 16th note passages slightly faster and with a softer sound.

Caprice No. 9: Allegretto

In the ninth caprice – traditionally nicknamed *La Caccia*, "The Hunt" – it is worth noting that in the ritornello passages, Paganini made specific indications for the violin to alternately imitate the sounds of the flute, "flauto," and the horn, "corno." In the contrasting E minor section (m.17), the changing articulations evoke a brilliant playfulness. In the A minor section (m.53), use a bold articulation to control the pace, achieving a rhythmically strong and steadfast atmosphere. In contrast, the 32nd note gestures should be fast, light, and almost ornamental. The ending is both gentle and tender.

Caprice No. 10: Vivace
Paganini's *martellato* indication suggests strong and persistent tonguing throughout. Nevertheless, it is important to maintain a linear "feel" and use the airstream to achieve long *legato* phrases, particularly when harmonic modulations occur in quick succession. The inclusion of large intervallic leaps, quick trills, and the overall *Vivace* tempo make this caprice extremely virtuosic and brilliant; therefore I have chosen to end with a flourish on the final note.

Caprice No. 11: Andante-Presto-Andante
The outer sections should be played with great lyricism and fluidity – a conscious *legato* sense that incorporates the grace notes into the melodic line. Although the expression is both romantic and gentle, it is important to adhere to the *Andante* marking and not let the tempo lag. Paganini implies the piece's vocal qualities with the indication, *il canto ben marcato e sostenuto*. The contrasting *Presto* section presents a challenge in triple-tonguing. In order to maintain a quick and lively line, slightly double-dot the first beat allowing as much space as possible at this tempo between the first, second, third and fourth notes (this is also useful for breathing). In contrast, use a light and skipping triple-tongue on the sextuplet passages, supported by enough pressure in the airstream to propel the line forward.

Caprice No. 12: Allegro
The challenge for the flutist in the twelfth caprice is to maintain the *Allegro* tempo with extreme flexibility of embouchure, so as to execute the piece with an ultimate *legato*. Be certain to observe the phrasing and accent markings in order to bring out the rhythmic variety, and utilize these markings as a guide for breathing choices.

Caprice No. 13: Allegro
The thirteenth caprice, traditionally nicknamed *La risata del diavolo*, "The Devil's Laugh," evokes the violin with its double stops and glissandi. Its nickname, however, has given rise to great distortion in performance practice; instrumentalists commonly change tempi and add pauses and articulations that are distant from Paganini's original indications. To achieve a violinistic sense of phrasing, use very quick grace notes in the opening gesture and, in the following passage (m.5-6), light triple-tonguing while following the *crescendo* and *decrescendo* markings. In the *Minore* section, a heavier and fuller sound can be used to support the downward octave leaps.

Caprice No. 14: Moderato
The chordal nature of the original violin writing gives this caprice a rich, sonorous quality. To achieve this character, it is important that the flute articulation be simultaneously separate and long, accenting the melodic line and using the grace notes to outline the harmonic progression. Although the manuscript does not give an initial dynamic indication, I have opted for a *forte* to capture the fullness of the violin double stops. In m.9, I have added a *piano* with *crescendo* for four measures that corresponds to the harmonic progression. After m.23, all dynamics reflect the original manuscript.

Caprice No. 15: Posato
Try to accentuate the melody (beginning at m.8) as outlined by the first note of every 32nd note group while maintaining the indicated dynamics. By contrast, the *staccato* passages after m.19 should be strong and forward-moving with full support for the high notes as well as the large leaps to the bottom octave.

Caprice No. 16: Presto
For the violin, the almost manic drive in the sixteenth caprice is generated by bow control. For the flute, however, the wildness and energy comes from maintaining a strong, full sound, confident, relentless articulation, a *Presto* tempo, and using the flute's full range. Paganini's insistence on fortes on downbeats and offbeats (translated as flute accents) helps further ground the piece, allowing for excitement and boldness in its execution.

Caprice No. 17: Sostenuto-Andante

The introduction should be played with a flourish and a well-connected *legato*, ending with a strong sound at the B-flats in m.4. By contrast, the *Andante* section can have a more graceful and elegant character with a light and shimmering tone on the trilled eighth note gestures. In the *Minore* section (m.26) broad double-tonguing should be used to intensify both the linear "feel" and the dramatic temperament.

Caprice No. 18: Corrente

Paganini specifies that the outer parts be played entirely on the G string, creating an almost hunt-like, bugle call character for the *Corrente*. For the flute, the most natural adaptation seemed an initially sparing use of harmonics, gradually increased with every repetition to evoke the natural world of the overtone series. By contrast, the *Minore* section is quick and brilliant; a *legato* slur between the first and second notes of the scale increases the speed of the scales.

Caprice No. 19: Lento-Allegro assai

In the introduction, keep the emphasis on the lower octave while imitating the richness of the original violin double stops, achieved by maintaining an extreme *legato* on the grace note octave jumps. By contrast, the *Allegro* section should be light and playful with the *Minore* exuding a sense of drama and urgency, particularly in the passages marked *piano*.

Caprice No. 20: Allegretto

The opening section should have a very sustained, lyrical feeling, the repeated low D grace notes imitating a drone. When repeated up the octave (m.17), the main phrase should retain this feeling as much as possible despite the faster note values and large intervallic leaps. As a result of the varied articulations, the B minor section (m.25) should generate a dramatic sense of power and determination as well as capriciousness.

Caprice No. 21: Amoroso-Presto

In the original version, the introductory measures simply outline a two-octave jump on A. Therefore the flute embellishments should maintain a restricted dynamic level, and emphasis should be placed on matching the two outside notes as closely as possible. The beautiful *Amoroso* melody (to be played *con espressione*) should be simple and sung, with the flourishes at the ends of the phrases (e.g., m.10) likewise retaining the *dolce* character of the line. In contrast, the *Presto* passage requires light and quick double-tonguing and special care not to become shrill in the higher register.

Caprice No. 22: Marcato

In this caprice, we have an opportunity to address airstream speed, using support to achieve a beautiful *legato* between the opening octaves. The original writing (e.g., m.3) calls for light, bouncy violin double stops. To obtain a similar, playful quality, make use of the two-note articulation wherever possible. The *Minore* section challenges articulation and necessitates a focus on the flexibility of the lips, particularly in the pedal notes (e.g., m.33).

Caprice No. 23: Posato

This caprice is bold, broad, and powerful. It is characterized by clear articulation, full sound, and great rhythmic stability regardless of register. While the tempo remains the same in the Minore section, attention shifts to the rhythmic subdivisions, giving the music a sense of motion and character. The flutist should aim for great clarity in the *staccato* notes to create a fleeting, rippling sonority in the fast groups of 64th notes.

Caprice No. 24: Tema con Variazioni (Quasi Presto)

Arguably the most famous of the 24, the final caprice has been subject to the greatest number of transcriptions and variations. Therefore I have allowed myself some departures from the manuscript in order to use the flute in a more idiomatic manner.

Despite the control and firmness of rhythm, the theme is marked *piano*. Although this is changed to a *forte* in Variation 1, it would be advisable to keep the tonguing and general spirit light throughout the grace notes. While I have tried to hint at the sense of complexity and duality created by the original octaves in Variation 3, I opted to transform the character altogether by using harmonics. The fundamentals on the bottom line are only suggestions; the flutist is free to choose those best suited to him or herself. Variation 4 should be played *piano* but with a warm and connected sound throughout the high register. In Variation 6, I have incorporated some optional flutter-tonguing into the trills, adding fire and vibrancy to what were originally parallel thirds. Even when not fluttering, keep the notes connected with the airstream. In Variation 8, I added harmonics to give the high notes a more shimmering sound and greater contrast with the bass. Variation 9 uses the flute's top register to generate great brilliance, later contrasted by the quiet *legato* in Variation 10. For Variation 11, I drew on the powerhouse spirit of Lizst's piano transcription and the excellent variations for flute and piano by Lambros D. Callimahos. The Finale should be fiery, brilliant, and rich.

Marina Piccinini

4

Moderato

No. 2

dolce e leggiero　　　　　　　*sim.*

6

No. 3

ED30116

No. 4 Maestoso

ED30116

(This page intentionally left blank to facilitate page turns)

12

No. 6

Lento

sempre legato*

cresc.

smorzando

cresc.

* Always play the melody note first, with a light articulation,
then slur into the tremolo. Tremolos are not measured.

18

20

Allegretto "La Caccia"

No. 9

dolce

Vivace

No. 10

ED30116

24

26

Allegro non troppo "La Risata del Diavolo"

No. 13

Fine

Minore

D.C. al Fine

No. 15

D.C. al Fine

Presto

No. 16

ED30116

34

Fine

Minore

D.S. al Fine
senza replica

36

Corrente

No. 18

Allegro

38

No. 19

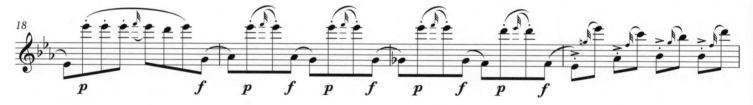

40

D.C. al Fine

42

No. 21

Amoroso

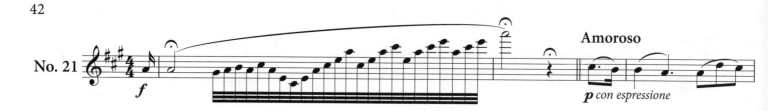

Presto

Marcato

No. 22

D.C. al Fine

(This page intentionally left blank to facilitate page turns)

No. 23

Posato

Minore

dim.

cresc.

p   f   p   f

D. C. al Fine

48

Tema con Variazioni (Quasi Presto)

ED30116

Var. VIII

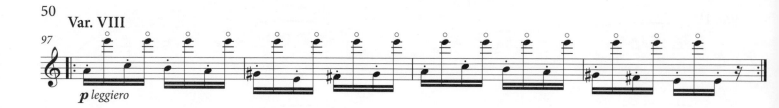

Var. IX

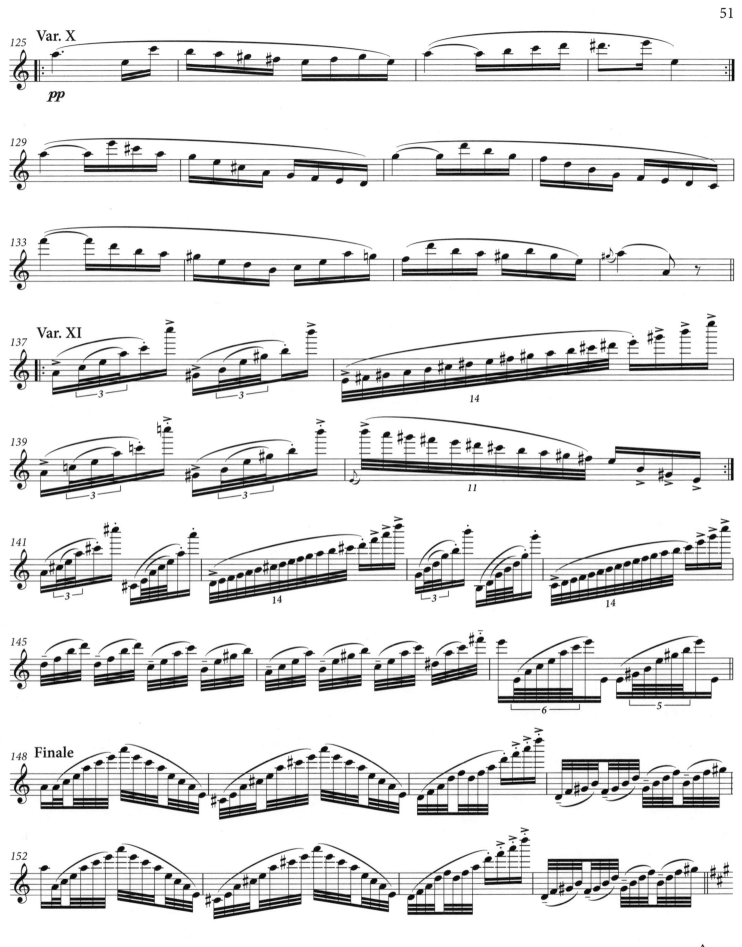